EL SALVADOR

CONTENTS

CORE EXPECTATIONS FOR PEACE CORPS VOLUNTEERS

In working toward fulfilling the Peace Corps mission of promoting world peace and friendship, as a trainee and Volunteer, you are expected to do the following:

1. Prepare your personal and professional life to make a commitment to serve abroad for a full term of 27 months

2. Commit to improving the quality of life of the people with whom you live and work and, in doing so, share your skills, adapt them, and learn new skills as needed

3. Serve where the Peace Corps asks you to go, under conditions of hardship if necessary, and with the flexibility needed for effective service

4. Recognize that your successful and sustainable development work is based on the local trust and confidence you build by living in, and respectfully integrating yourself into, your host community and culture

5. Recognize that you are responsible 24 hours a day, 7 days a week for your personal conduct and professional performance

6. Engage with host country partners in a spirit of cooperation, mutual learning, and respect

7. Work within the rules and regulations of the Peace Corps and the local and national laws of the country where you serve

8. Exercise judgment and personal responsibility to protect your health, safety, and well-being and that of others

9. Recognize that you will be perceived, in your host country and community, as a representative of the people, cultures, values, and traditions of the United States of America

10. Represent responsively the people, cultures, values, and traditions of your host country and community to people in the United States both during and following your service

PEACE CORPS/EL SALVADOR
HISTORY AND PROGRAMS

History of the Peace Corps in El Salvador

The Peace Corps was invited to El Salvador and sent its first Volunteers in 1962. During the next 15 years, more than 1,500 Volunteers worked in 15– 20 sectors, serving primarily as project partners to government agencies and offices. In 1980, increasing violence prior to the civil war led the Peace Corps to close its offices. The destruction of economic and social infrastructure during the war sent El Salvador back to 1950s levels in most economic and social indicators. A 1986 earthquake destroyed much of what the war did not, especially in San Salvador. Moreover, widespread migration led to the breakdown of many social and family institutions and particularly affected youth and the environment.

The government of El Salvador invited the Peace Corps to return to El Salvador in 1993. The first Volunteers arrived later that year. They were asked to increase the capacity of local people in several priority areas identified by the government and later affirmed by civil society in the Plan de Nación, or National Plan, presented in 2000. The National Plan is a blueprint for national development, and Peace Corps programming is consistent with its priorities. The role of Peace Corps Volunteers remains to build capacity for local people and institutions.

History and Future of Peace Corps Programming in El Salvador

Currently, Peace Corps/El Salvador Volunteers serve in two primary project areas: community organization and economic development (COED) and youth development (YD).

COED Volunteers work with local governments to improve service delivery to citizens and increase citizen participation. Volunteers assigned to community organizations assist in meeting the public- service demands of the communities, while helping communities to articulate their needs to their municipal representatives. Volunteers are also introducing disaster planning and mitigation techniques to their communities to better prepare them for crisis situations arising from natural disasters.

Youth Development Volunteers collaborate with youth leaders and local institutions as part of an integrated approach to address issues of youth development. Volunteers promote activities for youth to expand their critical thinking ability, foster their capacity to make sound decisions, and demonstrate moral, social, emotional, physical, and cognitive competence. The project is designed to address challenges youth face both in the home and at work to help them develop the knowledge, skills, and attitudes to become active, contributing members of their communities.

Volunteers in all projects are also involved in crosscutting themes, including gender awareness, HIV/AIDS education, environmental education, English, and information technology. In addition, Volunteers undertake myriad secondary projects in the communities where they live and work. In all of these projects and activities, Volunteers' project partners are government and nongovernmental organizations (NGOs) and people from the community. As always, the Peace Corps' efforts are focused on the less fortunate.

COUNTRY OVERVIEW:
EL SALVADOR AT A GLANCE

History

Like most of Central America, El Salvador's history is marked by conquest and turbulence. Its early indigenous people were the Pipils, members of a war-like tribe from Central Mexico who resembled the Aztecs more than the Mayans. After Pedro de Alvarado conquered the region, centuries of Spanish domination followed. There was little gold and few precious minerals within the territory that is now El Salvador, but its agricultural abundance was quickly recognized, and a series of agricultural crops have dominated its economic history: cacao, indigo, coffee, cotton, and sugar cane.

El Salvador was a leader in the movement to integrate the five Central American countries. In 1823, it helped found the United Provinces of Central America and even once petitioned the United States for statehood. In 1838, after regional rivalries and conflicts doomed integration, it became a republic.

El Salvador's early history as an independent state was marked by frequent revolutions. It wasn't until the period of 1900–30 that relative stability was achieved. The economic elite ruled the country in conjunction with the military, and the power structure was controlled by a relatively small number of wealthy landowners. From 1932—the year of General Maximiliano Hernández Martinez's coup following his brutal suppression of rural resistance—until 1980, all but one Salvadoran president was an army officer. Periodic presidential elections were seldom free or fair.

The 1980s, known as El Salvador's "lost decade," was dominated by war and social upheaval. The fighting ended with the signing of the United Nations-brokered 1992 Peace Accords, and the country is now considered by many as a model for moving beyond war and oppression to peace and democracy. Economic development, however, is still a distant dream, and inequities still restrict access to many rights and services.

Government

El Salvador is a democratic republic governed by a president and an 84-member unicameral Legislative Assembly. The president is elected by direct popular vote and serves for a five-year term by absolute majority vote. A second-round runoff is required if no candidate receives more than 50 percent of the first-round vote. Members of the Assembly, also elected by popular vote, serve for three-year terms. The country has an independent judiciary and supreme court.

Economy

The Salvadoran economy continues to benefit from a commitment to free markets and careful fiscal management. The impact of the civil war and subsequent natural disasters on El Salvador's economy has been devastating, and developing the conditions for economic growth remains the country's greatest challenge. Its traditional agricultural crops are suffering from low prices and productivity. The number of *maquilas* (assembly plants) is growing and providing some jobs, particularly to women, but wages are low and hours are long. The greatest source of economic assistance is from the estimated 2.5 million Salvadorans who live abroad (primarily in the United States) and send home approximately $2.8 billion annually.

People and Culture

El Salvador's population numbers about 6.9 million, of which 90 percent is of mixed Indian and Spanish descent. About 1 percent is indigenous; very few Indians have retained their customs and traditions. The country's people are largely Roman Catholic (although Protestant groups are growing), and Spanish is the language spoken by virtually all inhabitants. The capital city, San Salvador, has about 2.2 million people; an estimated 40 percent of El Salvador's population lives in rural areas.

Environment

The state of the environment in El Salvador poses a critical threat to national health and economic growth. There is virtually no uncontaminated surface water in the country. Agricultural runoff, untreated human waste, and industrial discharge increasingly pollute groundwater. Native forest exists only in several small, protected areas, and the effects of deforestation contributed greatly to hundreds of landslides that occurred during recent earthquakes. Air and noise pollution are growing concerns, especially in crowded urban areas. El Salvador's struggling Ministry of Natural Resources is understaffed and inefficient.

RESOURCES FOR FURTHER INFORMATION

Following is a list of websites for additional information about the Peace Corps and El Salvador and to connect you to returned Volunteers and other invitees. Please keep in mind that although the Peace Corps try to make sure all these links are active and current, it cannot be guaranteed . If you do not have access to the Internet, visit your local library. Libraries offer free Internet usage and often let you print information to take home.

A note of caution: As you surf the Internet, be aware that you may find bulletin boards and chat rooms in which people are free to express opinions about the Peace Corps based on their own experience, including comments by those who were unhappy with their choice to serve in the Peace Corps. These opinions are not those of the Peace Corps or the U.S. government, and we hope you will keep in mind that no two people experience their service in the same way.

General Information About El Salvador

www.lonelyplanet.com/destinations
Visit this site for general travel advice about almost any country in the world.

www.state.gov

The Department of State's website issues background notes periodically about countries around the world. Find El Salvador and learn more about its social and political history. You can also go to the site's international travel section to check on conditions that may affect your safety.

www.geography.about.com/library/maps/blindex.htm
This online world atlas includes maps and geographical information, and each country page contains links to other sites, such as the Library of Congress, that contain comprehensive historical, social, and political background.

www.cyberschoolbus.un.org/infonation/info.asp
This United Nations site allows you to search for statistical information for member states of the U.N.

Connect With Returned Volunteers and Other Invitees

www.rpcv.org
This is the site of the National Peace Corps Association, made up of returned Volunteers. On this site you can find links to all the Web pages of the "Friends of" groups for most countries of service, comprised of former Volunteers who served in those countries. There are also regional groups that frequently get together for social events and local volunteer activities.

www.PeaceCorpsWorldwide.org
This site is hosted by a group of returned Volunteer writers. It is a monthly online publication of essays and Volunteer accounts of their Peace Corps service.

Online Articles/Current News Sites About El Salvador

www.elsalvador.com
This site is from one of the two most visible newspapers in El Salvador.

www.laprensagrafica.com
This is a popular newspaper in El Salvador.

International Development Sites About El Salvador

elsalvador.usaid.gov/
USAID El Salvador

Recommended Books

1. Anderson, Thomas R. *El Salvador, 1932.* EDUCA, Centroamérica, 1976.

2. *El Salvador Imágenes para no olvidar 1900-1999.* Asociación Equipo Maíz, 1999.

3. *El Salvador, 10 años después...Una historia revelada 1992-2002.* Asociación Equipo Maíz, 2001.

4. Lardé y Larín , Jorge. *El Salvador: Inundaciones e Incendios, Erupciones y Terremotos.* Dirección de Publicaciones e Impresos, Consejo Nacional para la Cultura y el Arte, CONCULTURA San Salvador, 2000.

5. Browning, David. *El Salvador, la tierra y el hombre.* Ministerio de Educación. Dirección de Publicaciones, 1975.

Books About the History of the Peace Corps

1. Hoffman, Elizabeth Cobbs. *All You Need is Love: The Peace Corps and the Spirit of the 1960s.* Cambridge, Mass.: Harvard University Press, 2000.

2. Rice, Gerald T. *The Bold Experiment: JFK's Peace Corps.* Notre Dame, Ind.: University of Notre Dame Press, 1985.

3. Stossel, Scott. *Sarge: The Life and Times of Sargent Shriver.* Washington, D.C.: Smithsonian Institution Press, 2004.

4. Meisler, Stanley. *When the World Calls: The Inside Story of the Peace Corps and its First 50 Years.* Boston, Mass.: Beacon Press, 2011.

Books on the Volunteer Experience

1. Dirlam, Sharon. *Beyond Siberia: Two Years in a Forgotten Place.* Santa Barbara, Calif.: McSeas Books, 2004.

2. Casebolt, Marjorie DeMoss. *Margarita: A Guatemalan Peace Corps Experience.* Gig Harbor, Wash.: Red Apple Publishing, 2000.

3. Erdman, Sarah. *Nine Hills to Nambonkaha: Two Years in the Heart of an African Village.* New York, N.Y.: Picador, 2003.

4. Hessler, Peter. *River Town: Two Years on the Yangtze.* New York, N.Y.: Perennial, 2001.

5. Kennedy, Geraldine ed. *From the Center of the Earth: Stories out of the Peace Corps.* Santa Monica, Calif.: Clover Park Press, 1991.

6. Thompsen, Moritz. *Living Poor: A Peace Corps Chronicle.* Seattle, Wash.: University of Washington Press, 1997 (reprint).

LIVING CONDITIONS AND VOLUNTEER LIFESTYLE

Communications

Mail

Your temporary mailing address in El Salvador, while you are a trainee, will be as follows:

"Your Name," PCV
Apartado Postal 1947
Correo Nacional
Centro de Gobierno
San Salvador, El Salvador

Once you have been assigned to a site and sworn in as a Volunteer, you will be responsible for sending your site address to family and friends.

In general, the mail system between the United States and El Salvador is dependable. Airmail can take anywhere from 10 14 days to and from El Salvador; surface mail can take much longer (two to three months). Also, the farther you are from a large city, the less dependable the mail. Local mail couriers, such as Urgente Express or DHL, can be used to send/receive mail a bit faster; however, their service fees are much higher than those of the national post office.

Peace Corps/El Salvador recommends that you establish a regular schedule for communicating since friends and relatives in the United States may become concerned if they do not hear from you for an extended period of time. However, after Volunteers have sworn in and moved to their sites, communication habits change as they become more involved in projects and the novelty of their lifestyle wears off. A delay in the mail may also be the result of Volunteers being in a more isolated site.

Peace Corps/El Salvador does not recommend sending money, electronic devices, or airline tickets to Volunteers through the mail. It is usually not worth the effort to get packages from home. Airline tickets can be prepaid with the airline and someone in the United States can inform you of the reference number so you can pick up the ticket in San Salvador. Many Volunteers prefer to receive tickets via the e-ticket option. Customs duties may exceed the value of the items sent, and the time invested often means an entire day's travel to the city or airport.

Should it become necessary to have an item sent to you in El Salvador, it's recommended the items be limited to those that can fit in a padded envelope. Padded envelopes are usually not opened by customs officials and are taxed less than other types of packages. The express shipping company DHL International has an office in San Salvador. Packages may be sent to you in care of the Peace Corps office in El Salvador using this service. DHL can be costly and usually requires a phone number and street address. (Packages sent via an express carrier cannot be delivered to a post office box).

The street address of the Peace Corps Office is as follows:

Cuerpo de Paz/El Salvador
Avenida las Dalias No. 3
Condominio Petaluma
Colonia San Francisco
San Salvador, El Salvador
América Central

The phone number for the Peace Corps office in El Salvador is 011.503.2207.6000.

Telephones

The international phone service to and from El Salvador is very good. AT&T, Sprint, and MCI have direct-dial lines from El Salvador to the United States; however, their service is much more expensive than local long distance companies. The national telecommunication system has been privatized, so many local telephone companies offer very low rates when calling to the United States. Calls within the country are usually made from cellular telephones. Even very rural communities tend to have access to cellular telephone service. Many Volunteers purchase cellphones for their personal use. If you have a cellular telephone from the States, and it has an interchangeable SIM chip, you may be able to use it here in El Salvador.

Computer, Internet, and Email Access

Email and Internet access are more common and widespread and are frequently used by Volunteers, although travel may be required to find Internet cafes. Still, every regional department has Internet facilities, so access to the Internet is never more than two hours away and often closer. Some Volunteers have their laptops here and appreciate having brought them. This depends on your personal interest, as it is seldom a necessity for your eventual work here.

Please be aware that the climate in El Salvador may ruin some of your belongings. For this reason, do not bring things you cannot risk losing due to theft, loss, moisture, etc. The Peace Corps does not provide insurance coverage for your personal effects, although you may purchase insurance for your belongings. Ultimately, you are responsible for the safekeeping of your personal belongings. The Peace Corps cannot reimburse you for losses or damage.

Housing and Site Location

Peace Corps trainees are not assigned to individual sites until the end of their pre-service training. This gives Peace Corps staff the opportunity to assess each trainee's technical and language skills prior to assigning sites, in addition to finalizing site selections with counterpart agencies. When speaking with your project manager, you will have the opportunity to provide input on your site preferences, including geographical location, distance from other Volunteers, work preferences, and/or living conditions. However, keep in mind that many factors influence the site selection process and the Peace Corps cannot guarantee placement where you might ideally like to be. Most Volunteers will live in small towns or in rural villages but will usually be within one hour of the nearest Volunteer. Some sites will require a six- to 10-hour bus ride from the capital city.

Living Allowance and Money Management

Volunteers are expected to live at the same level as the Salvadoran people in their community. They are given a moving-in allowance at the time of swearing in and receive a monthly stipend as Volunteers. The "living allowance" is to be used to cover daily expenses. Volunteers often wish to bring additional money for travel to other countries. Credit or debit cards are recommended for this. Traveler's checks can be used, but there is usually a small charge for cashing them at banks, and many businesses will not accept them. Lots of cash is not recommended because of the potential for theft. As a trainee, the training center will help you open a bank account at a local bank, where you will receive your trainee and Volunteer allowances and where you can deposit any cash or traveler's checks that you might bring.

Many Salvadoran businesses in the capital and larger cities accept credit cards, including Visa and MasterCard. Other major credit cards are accepted in the major cities, but not as frequently. The U.S. dollar is the official currency so there is no issue of currency exchange. You may find it advantageous to retain a U.S. checking account, particularly if you can convince your bank to waive service charges during your Peace Corps service.

Food and Diet

Food Availability: Food availability depends on the season and the size of the community and region you live in. Do not arrive in-country expecting to eat the food you ate at home. Come with an open mind about a new diet.

Fruit and Vegetables: Many local varieties of fruits and vegetables are available and generally of good quality, but it is virtually impossible to wash away all dirt and microorganisms from those vegetables with minute cracks and crevices, such as lettuce, celery, and cauliflower. In markets, these foods are exposed to a variety of flies and other germ-bearing insects, and are handled by numerous individuals unfamiliar with basic hygiene. In addition, vegetables are frequently freshened by sprinkling them with water that may be polluted. With this in mind, it becomes obvious that attention must be given to the selection and treatment of these foods prior to ingestion.

All fruits and vegetables that will not be peeled or cooked should be washed in soap and water (any dish detergent will do), rinsed in clean water, and soaked 20 minutes in a bleach-and-water solution. This method will eliminate much of the bacteria, but it is still less than 100- percent effective in destroying amoeba cysts.

Meat and Poultry: Many kinds of meat and poultry are available in the local market. Unlike similar products in the United States, they are not properly inspected, aged, or refrigerated. To avoid the risk of infection, meat and poultry must be thoroughly cooked.

Seafood: Seafood, particularly shellfish, carries germs and parasites if grown in contaminated waters. Diseases that can be transmitted by shellfish include typhoid fever, infectious hepatitis, and some types of dysentery. Eat only cooked fish and shellfish. Never eat raw fish or shellfish.

Dairy Products: Locally obtained "raw" milk should be boiled. Store-bought packaged milk and other milk products (e.g., butter, cheese, or ice cream), if pasteurized, are safe to consume. Non-pasteurized dairy products provide a favorable setting for many infectious organisms. All non-pasteurized milk should be brought to a roiling boil before drinking.

Food Storage: Heat and humidity cause foods to spoil rapidly. Prepare only what you will eat at one setting. Eliminate leftovers, particularly custards and puddings. Intestinal illness is often caused by spoiled foods. All foods should obviously be obtained as fresh as possible. It is best to store most foods in the refrigerator, covered in glass or plastic containers. Do not allow cooked food to stand uncovered. Handle food as little as possible.

Beverages: All water is considered unsafe for drinking and making ice. It should be boiled for at least one minute. Boiled water should be stored in clean glass containers, which are washed and rinsed frequently. Purified bottled water can only be purchased in larger cities.

Filters remove some of the larger microorganisms and microscopic material, providing aesthetically acceptable water. However, unless the filters are frequently removed, thoroughly washed with a brush, and boiled for 10 minutes, they act as a source of contamination. If filtering is used in conjunction with boiling, the safest procedure is to filter first and follow with boiling. Chlorine also may be used after filtering.

Volunteers contemplating local travel should carry their own purified water or obtain iodine water purification tablets from the health unit.

A variety of carbonated soft drinks is available in El Salvador. These drinks are generally safe because the carbonation process creates an environment unfavorable for the growth of bacteria. Coconut water is enjoyable to some and quite safe to drink. Hot coffee and tea are safe to drink, since the water has been boiled.

Stronger drinks served with ice should be avoided. Alcohol will not disinfect dirty ice. Moreover, many health authorities feel that alcohol is tolerated less in the tropics than in colder climates. Excessive and daily use can cause salt loss and dehydration, make you more susceptible to dysentery, and reduce your tolerance to stress, heat, and physical activity. As is well-known, excessive alcohol intake can be extremely damaging to your mental and physical health.

While it is very possible to be vegetarian and/or vegan, it will be a challenge and individuals will need to think through their personal strategy to maintain their diet. This also applies to people with special dietary conditions. In general, Salvadorans eat meat, eggs, and/or dairy at all meals and many deep- fried foods. Anything outside the basic common diet would have been taken care of by the Volunteer/trainee.

Transportation

Operation of privately owned vehicles by Volunteers is prohibited. Most urban travel is by bus or taxi. Rural travel ranges from buses to mini-buses, to trucks, to a lot of walking. On emergencies, a Volunteer may be asked to drive a sponsor's vehicle, but this is only with prior permission of the country director. Volunteers in El Salvador do not need to obtain an international driver's license.

Geography and Climate

El Salvador is a relatively small country. Covering 8,123 square miles, it is about the size of Massachusetts. The capital city is San Salvador. Mountains separate the country into three distinct regions: the southern coastal belt, the central valleys and plateaus, and the northern mountains. The climate is semitropical, with temperatures ranging from 60 100 degrees Fahrenheit. It is tropical on the coast and temperate in the highlands. There is a distinct wet season from May through October; November through April is considered the dry season.

Social Activities

The Salvadoran culture is warm and hospitable, and most Volunteers find that establishing relationships and participating in local activities are very rewarding. For additional pertinent information on social activities, refer to the later section containing letters from El Salvador Volunteers.

Professionalism, Dress, and Behavior

The dress standards required of trainees at staging, during training, and of Volunteers in the field reflect what the Peace Corps staff (both U.S. and Salvadoran alike) believes to be culturally acceptable for El Salvador. These standards also apply to appropriate dress on the job and in the capital.

Sport sandals or flip-flops, regardless of their cost, are not appropriate for men or women in professional settings. Shoes must be worn at all times. Visible body piercings, with the exception of earrings on women, should be removed. Shorts are not appropriate outside the home in most areas, especially around the training center. Camouflage or khaki army equipment, uniforms, and duffel bags should be avoided. Men should keep hair and beards short and neatly trimmed. Pony tails on men are unacceptable and facial hair should be neatly groomed. Shirts with collars are preferable to T-shirts. Women are strongly advised to wear bras at all times outside of the home. All trainees and Volunteers are advised to cover pre-existing tattoos whenever possible, as tattoos in El Salvador are commonly associated with gang-related activities.

For some projects, there is a need for more casual and durable clothes appropriate to fieldwork, such as boots, jeans, and work shirts. These clothes must be clean and mended, with no patches. The best advice is to follow the lead of the Salvadorans.

In general, casual skirts, dresses, and dress pants are acceptable attire for women. Lightweight pants are appropriate for some work and social occasions. Jeans (not torn) are commonly worn by men and women for social occasions and for some fieldwork situations. Trainees should pack at least two "professional" outfits for special occasions.

It is important to remember that your personal tastes and characteristics should be a deciding factor in what to bring. It is not necessary to change your entire wardrobe. You should base your decision on what to bring on your present wardrobe, the type of work you will be doing, and the recommendations here.

Personal Safety

More detailed information about the Peace Corps' approach to safety is contained in the Health Care and Safety section, but it is an important issue and cannot be overemphasized. As stated in the Volunteer Handbook, becoming a Peace Corps Volunteer entails certain safety risks. Living and traveling in an unfamiliar environment (oftentimes alone), having a limited understanding of local language and culture, and being perceived as well-off are some of the factors that can put a Volunteer at risk. Many Volunteers experience varying degrees of unwanted attention and harassment. Petty thefts and burglaries are not uncommon, and incidents of physical and sexual assault do occur, although most El Salvador Volunteers complete their two years of service without incident. The Peace Corps has established procedures and policies designed to help you reduce your risks and enhance your safety and security. These procedures and policies, in addition to safety training, will be provided once you arrive in El Salvador. Using these tools, you are expected to take responsibility for your safety and well-being.

Each staff member at the Peace Corps is committed to providing Volunteers with the support they need to successfully meet the challenges they will face to have a safe, healthy, and productive service. Volunteers and families are encouraged to look at the safety and security information on the Peace Corps website at **www.peacecorps.gov/safety**.

Messages about Volunteer health and Volunteer safety are included. There is a section titled Safety and Security in Depth. Among topics addressed are the risks of serving as a Volunteer, posts' safety support systems, and emergency planning and communications.

Because of the importance of community integration and your personal safety and security, you will be required to live with a host family throughout your two years of service. This is a new, mandatory and non-negotiable requirement for future Volunteers assigned to El Salvador. It is important for you to consider this before accepting the assignment. Living with a host family can be challenging as you adapt to the dynamics of family life, possibly with cramped living conditions, a multigenerational family unit, and limited privacy. However, the benefits are extensive in that it will enhance your safety and security, enable you to more rapidly gain language and cultural skills, and foster your integration into the community. You will be a more active participant in the local community, rather than being viewed as a short-term resident.

Serving in El Salvador requires you to make lifestyle adjustments and take precautions to minimize your safety risks. You will need to be aware of your surroundings, be wary of potential crime situations, and exercise good common sense about your personal belongings, where and when you walk, and what transportation you take. You will need to refrain from staying out after dark and returning home late at night. You will need to comply with restrictions placed on travel and transportation within El Salvador and other policies that exist to minimize risks to your safety. Sound judgment and professional, mature behavior are required of PC/El Salvador Volunteers.

Rewards and Frustrations

Although the potential for job satisfaction is quite high, like all Volunteers, you will encounter frustrations. Due to financial or other challenges, collaborating agencies do not always provide the support promised. The pace of work and life is slower than what most Americans are accustomed to, and many people are hesitant to change practices and traditions that are centuries old. For these reasons, the Peace Corps experience is often described as a series of emotional peaks and valleys that occur while you adapt to a new culture and environment.

You will be given a high degree of responsibility and independence in your work—perhaps more than in any other job you have had or will ever experience. Often you will find yourself in situations that require an ability to motivate yourself and your counterparts with little guidance from supervisors. You may work for months without seeing any visible impact and without receiving feedback on your work. Development is a slow process. Positive progress is often seen only after the combined efforts of several Volunteers over the course of many years. You must possess the self-confidence, patience, and vision to continue working toward long-term goals without seeing immediate results.

To approach and overcome these difficulties, you will need commitment, maturity, flexibility, open-mindedness, and resourcefulness. Service in Peace Corps/El Salvador is not an extension of "year-abroad" study. However, Salvadorans are hospitable, friendly, and warm people. The Peace Corps staff, your co-workers, and fellow Volunteers will support you during challenging times, as well as in moments of success. Judging by the experience of former Volunteers, the peaks are well worth the difficult times, and most Volunteers leave El Salvador feeling they have gained much more than they sacrificed during their service. If you are able to make the commitment to integrate into your community and work hard, you will be a successful Volunteer.

PEACE CORPS TRAINING

Pre-Service Training

Training is an essential part of your Peace Corps service. The goal is to give you enough skills and information to allow you to live and work effectively in El Salvador. In doing that, training builds upon the experiences and expertise you bring with you to the Peace Corps. You are expected to approach your training with an open mind, a desire to learn, and a willingness to become involved. Peace Corps trainees officially become Peace Corps Volunteers after successful completion of training.

The training you will receive at the outset and over the course of your service provides you the opportunity to learn new skills and practice them as they apply to El Salvador. You will receive training and orientation in components of language, cross-cultural communication, area studies, development issues, health and personal safety, and technical skills pertinent to your assignment. The skills you learn will serve as a foundation upon which you will build your experience and work together as a group. You will also have the chance to experience local culture and customs on your own during your stay with a host family and on various site visits.

During the first few days in-country, you will participate in an arrival orientation at a training facility. After this initial period, you will move in with a host family in a community near the training center. You will live with one host family for the duration of your pre-service training. The host family experience will help you bring some of the topics covered in training to life, and it will give you a chance to practice your new language skills and directly observe and participate in Salvadoran culture. You will be expected to take part in the meals and daily activities of your host family. If you invest yourself in this experience, it will prove to be a rich and positive one. You will be assisted and guided in your cultural adaptation and skills acquisition by members of the training staff. All staff members will work with you—individually as well as in groups—to help you adapt to the new culture and prepare yourself for your eventual assignment.

Technical Training

Technical training will prepare you to work in El Salvador by building on the skills you already have and helping you develop new skills in a manner appropriate to the needs of the country. The Peace Corps staff, El Salvador experts, and current Volunteers will conduct the training program. Training places great emphasis on learning how to transfer the skills you have to the community in which you will serve as a Volunteer.

Technical training will include sessions on the general economic and political environment in El Salvador and strategies for working within such a framework. You will review your technical sector's goals and will meet with the El Salvador agencies and organizations that invited the Peace Corps to assist them. You will be supported and evaluated throughout the training to build the confidence and skills you need to undertake your project activities and be a productive member of your community.

Language Training

As a Peace Corps Volunteer, you will find that language skills are key to personal and professional satisfaction during your service. These skills are critical to your job performance, they help you integrate into your community, and they can ease your personal adaptation to the new surroundings. Therefore, language training is at the heart of the training program. You must successfully meet minimum language requirements to complete training and become a Volunteer. El Salvador language instructors teach formal language classes three days a week in small groups of four to five people.

Your language training will incorporate a community-based approach. In addition to classroom time, you will be given assignments to work on outside of the classroom and with your host family. The goal is to get you to a point of basic social communication skills so you can practice and develop language skills further once you are at your site. Prior to being sworn in as a Volunteer, you will work on strategies to continue language studies during your service.

Cross-Cultural Training

As part of your pre-service training, you will live with a Salvadoran host family. This experience is designed to ease your transition to life at your site. Families go through an orientation conducted by Peace Corps staff to explain the purpose of pre-service training and to assist them in helping you adapt to living in El Salvador. Many Volunteers form strong and lasting friendships with their host families.

Cross-cultural and community development training will help you improve your communication skills and understand your role as a facilitator of development. You will be exposed to topics such as community mobilization, conflict resolution, gender and development, nonformal and adult education strategies, and political structures.

Health Training

During pre-service training, you will be given basic medical training and information. You will be expected to practice preventive health care and to take responsibility for your own health by adhering to all medical policies. Trainees are required to attend all medical sessions. The topics include preventive health measures and minor and major medical issues that you might encounter while in El Salvador. Nutrition, mental health, setting up a safe living compound, and how to avoid HIV/AIDS and other sexually transmitted infections (STIs) are also covered.

Safety Training

During the safety training sessions, you will learn how to adopt a lifestyle that reduces your risks at home, at work, and during your travels. You will also learn appropriate, effective strategies for coping with unwanted attention and about your individual responsibility for promoting safety throughout your service.

Additional Trainings During Volunteer Service

In its commitment to institutionalize quality training, the Peace Corps has implemented a training system that provides Volunteers with continual opportunities to examine their commitment to Peace Corps service while increasing their technical and cross-cultural skills. During service, there are usually three training events. The titles and objectives for those trainings are as follows:

- In-service training: *Provides an opportunity for Volunteers to upgrade their technical, language, and project development skills while sharing their experiences and reaffirming their commitment after having served for three months.*

- Midservice conference (done in conjunction with technical sector in-service): *Assists Volunteers in reviewing their first year, reassessing their personal and project objectives, and planning for their second year of service.*

- Close-of-service conference: *Prepares Volunteers for the future after Peace Corps service and reviews their respective projects and personal experiences.*

The number, length, and design of these trainings are adapted to country-specific needs and conditions. The key to the training system is that training events are integrated and interrelated, from the pre-departure orientation through the end of your service, and are planned, implemented, and evaluated cooperatively by the training staff, Peace Corps staff, and Volunteers.

YOUR HEALTH CARE AND SAFETY IN EL SALVADOR

The Peace Corps' highest priority is maintaining the good health and safety of every Volunteer. Peace Corps medical programs emphasize the preventive, rather than the curative, approach to disease. The Peace Corps in El Salvador maintains a clinic with a full-time medical officer, who takes care of Volunteers' primary health-care needs. Additional medical services, such as testing and basic treatment, are also available in El Salvador at local hospitals. If you become seriously ill, you will be transported either to an American-standard medical facility in the region or to the United States.

Health Issues in El Salvador

Major health problems among Peace Corps Volunteers in El Salvador are rare and are often the result of a Volunteer not taking preventive measures to stay healthy. The most common health problems are mostly minor ones that are also found in the United States, such as colds, diarrhea, constipation, skin infections, headaches, ear infections, dental problems, minor injuries, sexually transmitted infections (STIs), adjustment disorders, emotional problems, and alcohol abuse. These problems may be more frequent or compounded by life in El Salvador, because certain environmental factors here raise the risk and/or exacerbate the severity of illness and injuries.

The most common major health concerns in El Salvador are malaria, rabies, tuberculosis, dengue fever, typhoid, intestinal parasites, upper respiratory infections, hepatitis, and HIV/AIDS. Because malaria is endemic in El Salvador, anti-malarial medication is required. You will also be vaccinated against hepatitis A and B, typhoid, rabies, tetanus, diphtheria and influenza.

Many of these health concerns can be easily avoided by using common sense and following basic preventive practices.

Helping You Stay Healthy

The Peace Corps will provide you with all the necessary inoculations, medications, and information to stay healthy. Upon your arrival in El Salvador, you will receive a medical handbook. At the beginning of training, you will receive a medical kit with supplies to take care of mild illnesses and first aid needs. The contents of the kit are listed later in this chapter.

During pre-service training, you will have access to basic medical supplies through the medical officer. However, you will be responsible for your own supply of prescription drugs and any other specific medical supplies you require, as the Peace Corps will not order these items during training. Please bring a three-month supply of any prescription drugs you use, since they may not be available here and it may take several months for shipments to arrive.

You will have physicals at midservice and at the end of your service. If you develop a serious medical problem during your service, the medical officer in El Salvador will consult with the Office of Health Services in Washington, D.C. If it is determined that your condition cannot be treated in El Salvador, you may be sent out of the country for further evaluation and care.

Maintaining Your Health

As a Volunteer, you must accept considerable responsibility for your own health. Proper precautions will significantly reduce your risk of serious illness or injury. The adage "An ounce of prevention is worth a pound of cure" becomes extremely important in areas where diagnostic and treatment facilities are not up to the standards of the United States. The most important of your responsibilities in El Salvador is to take the following preventive measures:

Strict Adherence to Recommended Drug Regimen to Prevent Malaria

Malaria is endemic in most areas of the Peace Corps world. Malaria can be rapidly fatal. Therefore, it is extremely important to fully comply with the recommended drug regimen to prevent malaria. Peace Corps Volunteers who do not fully comply with the required preventive regimen may be administratively separated. Your medical officer will discuss specific recommendations for the prevention of malaria in your area.

Prompt reporting to the Medical Office of Any Possible Exposure to Rabies

Rabies is present in nearly all Peace Corps countries. Any possible exposure to a rabid animal must be reported immediately to the medical office. Rabies exposure can occur through animal bites, scratches from animals' teeth, and contact with animal saliva. Your medial officer will take into consideration many factors to decide the appropriate course of therapy necessary to prevent rabies. Rabies, if contracted, is 100 percent fatal. All necessary rabies immunizations will be given by the Peace Corps medical office.

Many illnesses that afflict Volunteers worldwide are entirely preventable if proper food and water precautions are taken. These illnesses include food poisoning, parasitic infections, hepatitis A, dysentery, Guinea worms, tapeworms, and typhoid fever. Your medical officer will discuss specific standards for water and food preparation in El Salvador during pre-service training.

Abstinence is the most effective way to prevent infection with HIV and other sexually transmitted infections. You are taking risks if you choose to be sexually active. To lessen risk, use a condom every time you have sex. Whether your partner is a host country citizen, a fellow Volunteer, or anyone else, do not assume this person is free of HIV/AIDS or other STIs. You will receive more information from the medical officer about this important issue.

Volunteers are expected to adhere to an effective means of birth control to prevent an unplanned pregnancy. Your medical officer can help you decide on the most appropriate method to suit your individual needs. Contraceptive methods are available without charge from the medical officer.

It is critical to your health that you promptly report to the medical office or other designated facility for scheduled immunizations, and that you let the medical officer know immediately of significant illnesses and injuries.

Women's Health Information

Pregnancy is treated in the same manner as other Volunteer health conditions that require medical attention but also have programmatic ramifications. The Peace Corps is responsible for determining the medical risk and the availability of appropriate medical care if the Volunteer remains in-country. Given the circumstances under which Volunteers live and work in Peace Corps countries, it is rare that the Peace Corps' medical and programmatic standards for continued service during pregnancy can be met.

If feminine hygiene products are not available for you to purchase on the local market, the Peace Corps medical officer in El Salvador will provide them. If you require a specific product, please bring a three-month supply with you.

Your Peace Corps Medical Kit

The Peace Corps medical officer will provide you with a kit that contains basic items necessary to prevent and treat illnesses that may occur during service. Kit items can be periodically restocked at the medical office.

Medical Kit Contents

Ace bandages

Adhesive tape

American Red Cross First Aid & Safety Handbook

Antacid tablets (Tums)

Antibiotic ointment (Bacitracin/Neomycin/Polymycin B)

Antiseptic antimicrobial skin cleaner (Hibiclens)

Band-Aids

Butterfly closures

Calamine lotion

Cepacol lozenges

Condoms

Dental floss

Diphenhydramine HCL 25 mg (Benadryl)

Insect repellent stick (Cutter)

Iodine tablets (for water purification)

Lip balm (Chapstick)

Oral rehydration salts

Oral thermometer (Fahrenheit)

Pseudoephedrine HCL 30 mg (Sudafed)

Robitussin-DM lozenges (for cough)

Scissors

Sterile gauze pads

Tetrahydrozaline eyedrops (Visine)

Tinactin (antifungal cream)

Tweezers

Before You Leave: A Medical Checklist

If there has been any change in your health—physical, mental, or dental—since you submitted your examination reports to the Peace Corps, you must immediately notify the Office of Medical Services. Failure to disclose new illnesses, injuries, allergies, or pregnancy can endanger your health and may jeopardize your eligibility to serve.

If your dental exam was done more than a year ago, or if your physical exam is more than two years old, contact the Office of Medical Services to find out whether you need to update your records. If your dentist or Peace Corps dental consultant has recommended that you undergo dental treatment or repair, you must complete that work and make sure your dentist sends requested confirmation reports or X-rays to the Office of Medical Services.

If you wish to avoid having duplicate vaccinations, contact your physician's office to obtain a copy of your immunization record and bring it to your pre-departure orientation. If you have any immunizations prior to Peace Corps service, the Peace Corps cannot reimburse you for the cost. The Peace Corps will provide all the immunizations necessary for your overseas assignment, either at your pre-departure orientation or shortly after you arrive in El Salvador. You do not need to begin taking malaria medication prior to departure.

Bring a three-month supply of any prescription or over-the-counter medication you use on a regular basis, including birth control pills. Although the Peace Corps cannot reimburse you for this three-month supply, it will order refills during your service. While awaiting shipment—which can take several months—you will be dependent on your own medication supply. The Peace Corps will not pay for herbal or nonprescribed medications, such as St. John's wort, glucosamine, selenium, or antioxidant supplements.

You are encouraged to bring copies of medical prescriptions signed by your physician. This is not a requirement, but they might come in handy if you are questioned in transit about carrying a three-month supply of prescription drugs.

If you wear eyeglasses, bring two pairs with you. If a pair breaks, the Peace Corps will replace them, using the information your doctor in the United States provided on the eyeglasses form during your examination. The Peace Corps discourages you from using contact lenses during your service to reduce your risk of developing a serious infection or other eye disease. Most Peace Corps countries do not have appropriate water and sanitation to support eye care with the use of contact lenses. The Peace Corps will not supply or replace contact lenses or associated solutions unless an ophthalmologist has recommended their use for a specific medical condition and the Peace Corps Office of Medical Services has given approval.

If you are eligible for Medicare, are over 50 years of age, or have a health condition that may restrict your future participation in health care plans, you may wish to consult an insurance specialist about unique coverage needs before your departure. The Peace Corps will provide all necessary health care from the time you leave for your pre-departure orientation until you complete your service. When you finish, you will be entitled to the post-service health-care benefits described in the Peace Corps Volunteer Handbook. You may wish to consider keeping an existing health plan in effect during your service if you think age or pre-existing conditions might prevent you from re-enrolling in your current plan when you return home.

Safety and Security in Depth

Serving as a Volunteer overseas entails certain safety and security risks. Living and traveling in an unfamiliar environment, a limited understanding of the local language and culture, and the perception of being a wealthy American are some of the factors that can put a Volunteer at risk. Property theft and burglaries are not uncommon. Incidents of physical and sexual assault do occur, although almost all Volunteers complete their two years of service without serious personal safety problems.

Beyond knowing that Peace Corps approaches safety and security as a partnership with you, it might be helpful to see how this partnership works. Peace Corps has policies, procedures, and training in place to promote your safety. We depend on you to follow those policies and to put into practice what you have learned. An example of how this works in practice—in this case to help manage the risk of burglary—follows:

- Peace Corps assesses the security environment where you will live and work
- Peace Corps inspects the house where you will live according to established security criteria
- Peace Corps provides you with resources to take measures such as installing new locks
- Peace Corps ensures you are welcomed by host country authorities in your new community
- Peace Corps responds to security concerns that you raise
- You lock your doors and windows
- You adopt a lifestyle appropriate to the community where you live
- You get to know neighbors
- You decide if purchasing personal articles insurance is appropriate for you
- You don't change residences before being authorized by Peace Corps
- You communicate concerns that you have to Peace Corps staff

Factors that Contribute to Volunteer Risk

There are several factors that can heighten a Volunteer's risk, many of which are within the Volunteer's control. By far the most common crime that Volunteers experience is theft. Thefts often occur when Volunteers are away from their sites, in crowded locations (such as markets or on public transportation), and when leaving items unattended.

Before you depart for El Salvador there are several measures you can take to reduce your risk:

- Leave valuable objects in the U.S.

- Leave copies of important documents and account numbers with someone you trust in the U.S.

- Purchase a hidden money pouch or "dummy" wallet as a decoy

- Purchase personal articles insurance

After you arrive in El Salvador, you will receive more detailed information about common crimes, factors that contribute to Volunteer risk, and local strategies to reduce that risk. For example, Volunteers in El Salvador learn to do the following:

- Choose safe routes and times for travel, and travel with someone trusted by the community whenever possible

- Make sure one's personal appearance is respectful of local customs

- Avoid high-crime areas

- Know the local language to get help in an emergency

- Make friends with local people who are respected in the community

- Limit alcohol consumption

As you can see from this list, you must be willing to work hard and adapt your lifestyle to minimize the potential for being a target for crime. As with anywhere in the world, crime exists in El Salvador. You can reduce your risk by avoiding situations that place you at risk and by taking precautions. Crime at the village or town level is less frequent than in the large cities; people know each other and generally are less likely to steal from their neighbors. Tourist attractions in large towns are favorite worksites for pickpockets.

The following are other security concerns in El Salvador of which you should be aware:

Physical and Sexual Assault

In El Salvador, Volunteers may be impacted by incidents of theft due to the current economic situation. As a Volunteer, you have to be willing to forego certain freedoms that you may take for granted; freedoms like going to a deserted beach or forest, going out alone at night, or walking alone on some roads. You must take precautions that you may not be accustomed to taking in your hometown or city. And even if you take those precautions, you may be a victim simply because somebody wants something and they think they can get it from you—items such as money, electronics, jewelry, a bicycle, a camera, an appliance, or clothes.

While whistles and exclamations may be fairly common on the street, this behavior can be reduced if you dress conservatively, abide by local cultural norms, and respond according to the training you will receive.

Staying Safe: Don't Be a Target for Crime

You must be prepared to take on a large degree of responsibility for your own safety. You can make yourself less of a target, ensure that your home is secure, and develop relationships in your community that will make you an unlikely victim of crime. While the factors that contribute to your risk in El Salvador may be different, in many ways you can do what you would do if you moved to a new city anywhere: Be cautious, check things out, ask questions, learn about your neighborhood, know where the more risky locations are, use common sense, and be aware. You can reduce your vulnerability to crime by integrating into your community, learning the local language, acting responsibly, and abiding by Peace Corps policies and procedures. Serving safely and effectively in El Salvador will require that you accept some restrictions on your current lifestyle.

Support from Staff

If a trainee or Volunteer is the victim of a safety incident, Peace Corps staff is prepared to provide support. All Peace Corps posts have procedures in place to respond to incidents of crime committed against Volunteers. The first priority for all posts in the aftermath of an incident is to ensure the Volunteer is safe and receiving medical treatment as needed. After assuring the safety of the Volunteer, Peace Corps staff response may include reassessing the Volunteer's worksite and housing arrangements and making any adjustments, as needed. In some cases, the nature of the incident may necessitate a site or housing transfer. Peace Corps staff will also assist Volunteers with preserving their rights to pursue legal sanctions against the perpetrators of the crime. It is very important that Volunteers report incidents as they occur, not only to protect their peer Volunteers, but also to preserve the future right to prosecute. Should Volunteers decide later in the process that they want to proceed with the prosecution of their assailant, this option may no longer exist if the evidence of the event has not been preserved at the time of the incident.

Crime Data for El Salvador

Crime data and statistics for El Salvador, which are updated yearly, are available at the following link: http://www.peacecorps.gov/countrydata/elsalvador. Please take the time to review this important information.

Few Peace Corps Volunteers are victims of serious crimes and crimes that do occur overseas are investigated and prosecuted by local authorities through the local courts system. If you are the victim of a crime, you will decide if you wish to pursue prosecution. If you decide to prosecute, the Peace Corps will be there to assist you. One of our tasks is to ensure you are fully informed of your options and understand how the local legal process works. The Peace Corps will help you ensure your rights are protected to the fullest extent possible under the laws of the country.

If you are the victim of a serious crime, you will learn how to get to a safe location as quickly as possible and contact your Peace Corps office. It's important that you notify Peace Corps staff as soon as you can so the Peace Corps can provide you with the help you need.

Volunteer Safety Support in El Salvador

The Peace Corps' approach to safety is a five-pronged plan to help you stay safe during your service and includes the following: information sharing, Volunteer training, site selection criteria, a detailed emergency action plan, and protocols for addressing safety and security incidents. El Salvador's in-country safety program is outlined below.

The Peace Corps/El Salvador office will keep you informed of any issues that may impact Volunteer safety through **information sharing**. Regular updates will be provided in Volunteer newsletters and in memorandums from the country director. In the event of a critical situation or emergency, you will be contacted through the emergency communication network. An important component of the capacity of Peace Corps to keep you informed is your buy-in to the partnership concept with the Peace Corps staff. It is expected that you will do your part in ensuring that Peace Corps staff members are kept apprised of your movements in-country so they are able to inform you.

Volunteer training will include sessions on specific safety and security issues in El Salvador. This training will prepare you to adopt a culturally appropriate lifestyle and exercise judgment that promotes safety and reduces risk in your home, at work, and while traveling. Safety training is offered throughout service and is integrated into the language, cross-cultural aspects, health, and other components of training. You will be expected to successfully complete all training competencies in a variety of areas, including safety and security, as a condition of service.

Certain **site selection criteria** are used to determine safe housing for Volunteers before their arrival. The Peace Corps staff works closely with host communities and counterpart agencies to help prepare them for a Volunteer's arrival and to establish expectations of their respective roles in supporting the Volunteer. Each site is inspected before the Volunteer's arrival to ensure placement in appropriate, safe, and secure housing and worksites. Site selection is based, in part, on any relevant site history; access to medical, banking, postal, and other essential services; availability of communications, transportation, and markets; different housing options and living arrangements; and other Volunteer support needs.

You will also learn about Peace Corps/ El Salvador's detailed **emergency action plan**, which is implemented in the event of civil or political unrest or a natural disaster. When you arrive at your site, you will complete and submit a site locator form with your address, contact information, and a map to your house. If there is a security threat, you will gather with other Volunteers in **El Salvador** at predetermined locations until the situation is resolved or the Peace Corps decides to evacuate.

Finally, in order for the Peace Corps to be fully responsive to the needs of Volunteers, it is imperative that Volunteers immediately report any security incident to the Peace Corps office. The Peace Corps has established **protocols for addressing safety and security incidents** in a timely and appropriate manner, and it collects and evaluates safety and security data to track trends and develop strategies to minimize risks to future Volunteers.

DIVERSITY AND CROSS-CULTURAL ISSUES

In fulfilling its mandate to share the face of America with host countries, the Peace Corps is making special efforts to assure that all of America's richness is reflected in the Volunteer corps. More Americans of color are serving in today's Peace Corps than at any time in recent history. Differences in race, ethnic background, age, religion, and sexual orientation are expected and welcomed among Volunteers. Part of the Peace Corps mission is to help dispel any notion that Americans are all of one origin or race and to establish that each of us is as thoroughly American as the other despite our many differences.

Diversity helps us accomplish that goal. In other ways, however, it poses challenges. In El Salvador, as in other Peace Corps host countries, Volunteers' behavior, lifestyle, background, and beliefs are judged in a cultural context very different from their own. Certain personal perspectives or characteristics commonly accepted in the United States may be quite uncommon, unacceptable, or even repressed in El Salvador.

Outside of El Salvador's capital, residents of rural communities have had relatively little direct exposure to other cultures, races, religions, and lifestyles. What people view as typical American behavior or norms may be a misconception, such as the belief that all Americans are rich and have blond hair and blue eyes. The people of El Salvador are justly known for their generous hospitality to foreigners; however, members of the community in which you will live may display a range of reactions to cultural differences that you present.

To ease the transition and adapt to life in El Salvador, you may need to make some temporary, yet fundamental compromises in how you present yourself as an American and as an individual. For example, female trainees and Volunteers may not be able to exercise the independence available to them in the United States, political discussions need to be handled with great care, and some of your personal beliefs may best remain undisclosed. You will need to develop techniques and personal strategies for coping with these and other limitations. The Peace Corps staff will lead diversity and sensitivity discussions during pre-service training and will be on call to provide support, but the challenge ultimately will be your own.

Overview of Diversity in El Salvador

The Peace Corps staff in El Salvador recognizes the adjustment issues that come with diversity and will endeavor to provide support and guidance. During pre-service training, several sessions will be held to discuss diversity and coping mechanisms. The Peace Corps looks forward to having male and female Volunteers from a variety of races, ethnic groups, ages, religions, and sexual orientations, and hope that you will become part of a diverse group of Americans who take pride in supporting one another and demonstrating the richness of American culture.

What Might a Volunteer Face?

Possible Issues for Female Volunteers

Machismo is pervasive throughout El Salvador. Strict gender roles exist, particularly in rural areas. Women frequently receive catcalls, especially in areas where they are not known. The more you are established in your site and known to your community, the less likely you will be hassled.

Traditional roles in rural areas often prevent women from doing physical work except carrying firewood, water, or supplies from the market. Generally, women in El Salvador have attended less formal schooling than men so it is difficult for them to be taken seriously on technical issues. Additionally, Salvadoran women are usually not comfortable in expressing their opinions openly. Decisions are traditionally made by men. Gender roles for outsiders are somewhat less strict, although female Volunteers may find that expressions of independence that may be the norm in the United States are not culturally appropriate in El Salvador.

Possible Issues for Volunteers of Color

As a Volunteer of color, you may be the only non-white Volunteer within a project or training group. As such, it is quite possible that you may be working and living among people with little or no experience or understanding of your culture. You may not receive the level of personal support from other Volunteers that you would like. Likewise, it may be a challenge to find diverse role models among the Peace Corps staff.

In El Salvador, African-American Volunteers may be referred to as *negro* or other titles considered derogatory in American culture. *Negro* is the word for black in Spanish and may not be intended as derogatory in El Salvador. Based upon false cultural stereotypes, you may be evaluated as less professionally competent than white Volunteers.

Salvadorans may expect Latin-American Volunteers to automatically assume different role patterns than white Volunteers or to interact socially with more ease. Likewise, Volunteers with Latino surnames may be expected to speak Spanish fluently, while language testers may expect Latin-American Volunteers to perform more proficiently on Spanish tests. Latin-American Volunteers may not be considered or perceived as being from the United States.

Salvadorans may project stereotyped behavior observed in films on Asian-American Volunteers (the "Kung Fu Syndrome"). In El Salvador, Asian Americans are often identified by their cultural heritage, not by their American citizenship. Asians are collectively labeled as *chinos* (Chinese), regardless of their particular ethnic background. Current or historical host country involvement with Asian countries, or the presence of Asian merchants in the community, may have an impact on how Asian-American Volunteers are perceived. Asian Americans may not be accepted as North American.

Possible Issues for Senior Volunteers

Senior Volunteers are advised to designate a power of attorney to manage all financial matters during service prior to leaving for El Salvador. It is important that senior Volunteers be aware of possible issues of inclusion and acceptance among Volunteer peers. Others in the Peace Corps community may have little understanding of, or respect for, the lives and experiences of senior Americans. Seniors may not share social or recreational interests and may not receive the personal support they desire from younger Volunteers. As a result, senior Volunteers may not feel comfortable sharing personal, sexual, or health concerns. On the other hand, they may find that younger Volunteers look to them for advice and support. Some senior Volunteers find this as a very enjoyable part of their experience, while others choose not to fill this role. Because of the cultural standards, senior Volunteers may command more respect from Salvadorans than younger Volunteers.

Senior Volunteers may need to be assertive in developing an effective individual approach to language learning. Also, where great variety in site placement exists, Peace Corps staff and senior Volunteers need to collaborate to identify those sites most appropriate for single or married older Volunteers.

Possible Issues for Gay, Lesbian, or Bisexual Volunteers

LGBT sexual orientation or identity is not accepted in much of Salvadoran society. Additionally, HIV/AIDS (VIH/Sida in Spanish) is a critical issue in El Salvador and, as in other countries in the region, HIV affects men who have sex with men (MSM) disproportionally. Volunteers also need to be aware that there has been a backlash against gay American men for supposedly bringing HIV to Latin America and this may present particular challenges for gay men in-country. LGBT Volunteers may not be able to be as open about their sexual orientation as is in the U.S. and are encouraged to carefully consider this fact in the context of Salvadoran culture, and with respect to their host community. In El Salvador, some civil liberties are often nonexistent or denied to members of the LGBT community.

Some Volunteers do find the Peace Corps to be a "coming out" experience, while others find it a "going back into the closet" one. Volunteers generally choose not to be "out" in their communities, but may be "out" to certain individuals with whom they have built trusting relationships. You may serve for two years without meeting another gay Volunteer. Like most Volunteers, you may have difficulties with the *machismo* in El Salvador. Lesbian and bisexual women should be prepared to field questions regarding boyfriends, marriage, and sex. Gay and bisexual men will be asked about girlfriends, and may find themselves in situations where local men brag about female conquests, objectify women, and catcall. It is a good idea to start formulating personal strategies to deal with these difficult realities. Please know that Peace Corps/El Salvador is here to support you and you can utilize staff and your Volunteer support network as needed.

Possible Religious Issues for Volunteers

While the predominant religion has traditionally been Catholic, there are more and more Christian religions appearing throughout El Salvador. It is not uncommon to find large portions of the population in some communities to be Evangelical. Other religions include Judaism and Mormonism. Some nonreligious Volunteers have actually started attending church on Sundays because that is where a large part of the community can be found together.

Possible Issues for Volunteers With Disabilities

As part of the medical clearance process, the Peace Corps Office of Health Services determined that you were physically and emotionally capable, with or without reasonable accommodations, to perform a full tour of Volunteer service in El Salvador without unreasonable risk of harm to yourself or interruption of service. The Peace Corps/El Salvador staff will work with disabled Volunteers to make reasonable accommodations for them in training, housing, jobsites, or other areas to enable them to serve safely and effectively.

Possible Issues for Married Volunteers

Probably the biggest concern with married Volunteers is the tendency to speak English all the time, thus putting up a possible wall between the married couple and the community.

FREQUENTLY ASKED QUESTIONS

How much luggage am I allowed to bring to El Salvador?

Most airlines have baggage size and weight limits and assess charges for transport of baggage that exceeds those limits. The Peace Corps has its own size and weight limits and will not pay the cost of transport for baggage that exceeds these limits. The Peace Corps' allowance is two checked pieces of luggage with combined dimensions of both pieces not to exceed 107 inches (length + width + height) and a carry-on bag with dimensions of no more than 45 inches. Checked baggage should not exceed 100 pounds total with a maximum weight of 50 pounds for any one bag.

Peace Corps Volunteers are not allowed to take pets, weapons, explosives, radio transmitters (shortwave radios are permitted), automobiles, or motorcycles to their overseas assignments. Do not pack flammable materials or liquids such as lighter fluid, cleaning solvents, hair spray, or aerosol containers. This is an important safety precaution.

What is the electric current in El Salvador?

The electric voltage is 110v, the same as in the United States.

How much money should I bring?

Volunteers are expected to live at the same level as the people in their community. You will be given a settling-in allowance and a monthly living allowance, which should cover your expenses. Volunteers often wish to bring additional money for vacation travel to other countries. Credit cards and traveler's checks are preferable to cash (though may incur a fee). If you choose to bring extra money, bring the amount that will suit your own travel plans and needs.

When can I take vacation and have people visit me?

Each Volunteer accrues two vacation days per month of service (excluding training). Leave may not be taken during training, the first three months of service, or the last three months of service, except in conjunction with an authorized emergency leave. Family and friends are welcome to visit you after pre-service training and the first three months of service as long as their stay does not interfere with your work. Extended stays at your site are not encouraged and may require permission from your country director. The Peace Corps is not able to provide your visitors with visa, medical, or travel assistance.

Will my belongings be covered by insurance?

The Peace Corps does not provide insurance coverage for personal effects; Volunteers are ultimately responsible for the safekeeping of their personal belongings. However, you can purchase personal property insurance before you leave. If you wish, you may contact your own insurance company; additionally, insurance application forms will be provided, and we encourage you to consider them carefully. Volunteers should not ship or take valuable items overseas. Jewelry, watches, radios, cameras, and expensive appliances are subject to loss, theft, and breakage, and in many places, satisfactory maintenance and repair services are not available.

Do I need an international driver's license?

Volunteers in El Salvador do not need an international driver's license because they are prohibited from operating privately owned motorized vehicles. Most urban travel is by bus or taxi. Rural travel ranges from buses and minibuses to trucks, bicycles, and lots of walking.

What should I bring as gifts for Salvadoran friends and my host family?

This is not a requirement. A token of friendship is sufficient. Some gift suggestions include knickknacks for the house; pictures, books, or calendars of American scenes; souvenirs from your area; hard candies that will not melt or spoil; or photos to give away.

Where will my site assignment be when I finish training and how isolated will I be?

Peace Corps trainees are not assigned to individual sites until after they have completed pre-service training. This gives Peace Corps staff the opportunity to assess each trainee's technical and language skills prior to assigning sites, in addition to finalizing site selections with their ministry project partners. You will have the opportunity to provide input on your site preferences, including geographical location, distance from other Volunteers, work preferences and living conditions. However, keep in mind that many factors influence the site selection process and that the Peace Corps cannot guarantee placement where you would ideally like to be. Most Volunteers live in small towns or in rural villages and are usually within one hour from another Volunteer. Some sites require a five- to six-hour drive from the capital. Peace Corps/El Salvador only operates in the northern region of the country.

How can my family contact me in an emergency?

The Peace Corps Counseling and Outreach Unit provides assistance in handling emergencies affecting trainees and Volunteers or their families. Before leaving the United States, instruct your family to notify the Counseling and Outreach Unit immediately if an emergency arises, such as a serious illness or death of a family member. During normal business hours, the number for the Counseling and Outreach Unit is 855.855.1961 ext. 1470. After normal business hours and on weekends and holidays, the COU duty officer can be reached at the above number. For non-emergency questions, your family can get information from your country desk staff at the Peace Corps by calling 855.855.1961.

Can I call home from El Salvador?

The international phone service to and from El Salvador has improved tremendously in the last few years. AT&T, Sprint, and MCI can be accessed, but most Volunteers call from their cellphones.

Should I bring a cellular phone with me?

It is best to wait and see if there is coverage in your site and then decide if you want to buy a cellphone here. There are several companies, the phones are relatively cheap, and almost all Volunteers have bought them here. If you already have a cellphone, you might bring it with you. Many phones with a removable SIM chip can be reprogrammed by buying a local company's cellphone SIM chip and inserting it into the phone.

Will there be email and Internet access? Should I bring my computer?

Email and Internet access are becoming more common and widespread and frequently used by the Volunteers, although they may need to travel a bit to access such service. Every regional department has Internet facilities so email is never more than two hours away and oftentimes closer. Most Volunteers have their laptops here and appreciate having brought them. This mainly depends on your personal interest, as it is seldom a necessity for your eventual work here.

WELCOME LETTERS FROM
EL SALVADOR VOLUNTEERS

Buen día, amigos—

I want to tell you about my hands.

They are busy.

Busier than I could have imagined three months ago when I arrived in El Salvador. Busy kneading the dough of daily life—basic chores that we forget about in the U.S. because we've found ways around them. Stripping clothes from the lines when it starts to rain. Molding adobe bricks for the new house around the bend. Grinding corn and slapping out tortillas. Making soap from the pits of local avocados and olives. Clear-cutting a hillside with a machete to prepare for the crops. Gathering fruit from trees and nuts from the ground. Shooing the chicken off the bed again. Dipping buckets into cold water and bathing breathlessly.

And, more than anything, shaking other hands. My hands are busy shaking others, embracing everyone I meet as if it were my job. Because it is: I am a community organization and economic development (COED) Volunteer in a rural, mountaintop village, and, like every Peace Corps Volunteer, it is my central duty to grow as interwoven with my community as my little heart will allow.

You'll hear a lot about assimilation during training, and receive dozens of professional and personal reasons why it's the key to a safe, fulfilling experience. But, hopefully, you won't need to be convinced. Hopefully, you're sitting in your home right now swallowing hard with excitement at the thought of losing yourself into the swirls of a Central American hamlet. If so, you will find this country deeply receptive to you—ready to jaunt down the hill and across the plaza just to shake your hand back.

Then there's the work. Don't worry: There will be plenty of good stuff, the type of things your parents can glow about to others in the grocery line. I can't give you specifics, because your actual projects will depend more on the reality of your village at the moment you arrive than the name of your Peace Corps program. But I can say this: You will be working directly with villagers. You will be listening a lot, and trusting even more. You will be learning. And you will be helping community members realize just how many things they are already doing *right*.

If you want, you can create your own projects—fun youth classes, for example, that will fill the hours and build deeper layers of connection to the community. But in terms of sustainable development work, it is more about what you *don't* do but gently make sure gets done that will have the lasting impact. Most Salvadorans are hard-working, talented individuals already: Your role is to listen to them, perhaps broaden their vision a bit, and then help their talents and self-assurance bloom even more fully.

But you will gather all those details with time. For now, know this: The core of your experience will be something much more basic and challenging than the professional stuff. The core of your experience—as so many older Volunteers have assured me—will be about learning how to breathe a little more peacefully, and re-learning how to be a heartfelt neighbor and friend.

These are not always easy lessons. While this culture *overflows* with things that are effortless to love, there are others that are less so. Every day you'll find reasons to complain: the machismo façades, the dragging out of projects, the lack of privacy, and more.

But the beauty happens when you choose not to. The wide-eyed, soul-filling beauty happens when you realize afresh what an honor it is to be here, rising each morning to arms, homes, and hearts that are open to you anew. By joining the Peace Corps, you will be accepting this honor, accepting the opportunity to fall into this local rhythm, to learn from and embrace the people of this nation. And—in whatever behind-the-scenes, facilitative way you can—to offer yourself to their journey forward.

In the end, there are many different ways to love the world. For the next two years, this is mine.

So glad you chose the same!

Clayton Kennedy
COED Volunteer, 2010–12

Dear Peace Corps Invitee,

Congratulations on being invited to join the Peace Corps/El Salvador team! You've taken the first step toward a great adventure!

Who am I? My name is Edward Piersa, and I have been a Volunteer in El Salvador since March 2011 (I began PST 1 in January 2011). It has not been an easy journey between adjusting to cultural differences and learning a second language, but it has been well worth the ride so far. I remember how excited I was when I found myself in your position, but I really had no idea what to expect either.

The first thing I remember doing when I received my invitation was to call my closest family members and friends to tell them the news. The second was to rush back home from my P.O. Box and research as much as I could about El Salvador (in addition to reading all of the invitation documents themselves). One of the most helpful Peace Corps booklets that I personally found reading contained the letters from currently serving Peace Corps Volunteers in El Salvador.

So what exactly should you expect from El Salvador? Well, you may have already heard this before, but the truth is each experience is quite different. It often depends on what you make of it (like anything in life); therefore, I can only speak from my own experience, which has been extremely fulfilling at times and maddeningly frustrating at other times.

My best advice is this: Try to be as open-minded and patient as possible. Dealing with culture shock and language barriers is quite normal when moving to another country. Please realize that the culture of El Salvador (despite its crime problems) is usually quite friendly and giving. You will quickly feel like a part of your new community here, which is a real credit to El Salvador.

Enjoy the food (pupusas!) and *tranquilo* atmosphere of your new home. Much of the Peace Corps experience is as much about integrating yourself into your new site as it is about working with its members on community projects. Try to always remember that, especially during your first few months here.

As far as the projects themselves are concerned, I have personally found a lot of success with sports clubs (basketball and softball). There is always a demand for learning English here, so teaching English classes is a great way to satisfy a community´s need and integrate oneself into said community at the same time. On the other hand, an uphill battle here has been trying to achieve sustainable success with our town´s environment group; however, that doesn´t mean that these projects haven´t been worthwhile either.

Best of luck!

Sincerely,

Edward Piersa
COED Volunteer, 2011–13

PACKING LIST

This list has been compiled by Volunteers serving in El Salvador and is based on their experience. Use it as an informal guide in making your own list, bearing in mind that each experience is individual. There is no perfect list! You obviously cannot bring everything on the list, so consider those items that make the most sense to you personally and professionally. You can always have things sent to you later. As you decide what to bring, keep in mind that you have an 100-pound weight limit on baggage. And remember, you can get almost everything you need in El Salvador.

General Clothing

Individual tastes influence your decision of what will be useful and/or is not necessary. Site and work assignments vary as much as Salvadoran climate zones. This list should be used as a guide and provides only suggestions on what to bring. Salvadorans emphasize cleanliness and neatness and you may be judged by your appearance. Salvadorans, especially those in rural areas, dress more conservatively than North Americans. It is not necessary to change your entire wardrobe. Most Volunteers wear clothes similar to what they were used to wearing Stateside. If in doubt, minimize your clothes to the basics. Additional clothing and shoes are available in El Salvador and you may have well-tailored clothes made for you at rock-bottom prices. Also keep in mind that shoes sized over 8 for women and 11 for men are difficult to find.

Cotton fabrics and darker-colored clothing is recommended (darker colors hide dirt better). Since most clothes in the campo (countryside) are washed by hand on hard surfaces and hung to dry on rope or barbed wire, bring clothes that can withstand these rigors. Clothing with elastic, especially underwear, stretches rather quickly due to hand washing.

Bottoms
- 2–5 pairs of jeans, cotton pants, dark khakis (linen pants may be more comfortable and easier to wash/dry)
- 1–2 pairs of dress pants (khakis)
- 2–3 pairs of long shorts (capris for women)
- Skirts/dresses (casual, lightweight, knee-length or longer)
- Outfit for swearing-in ceremony (this is a semiformal event, but also a time to have some fun with dressing up)

Note: Jeans can be very heavy and hot. Lightweight, quick-drying pants are more practical. Shorts are not generally worn outside of the home in El Salvador, and wearing short shorts is certain to attract unwanted attention.

Tops
- T-shirts
- Polo style/golf shirts
- Blouses
- 1–2 dress shirts
- Tank tops (conservative)
- Fleece jacket and a lightweight jacket/rain jacket

Note: The nature of the weather here makes raingear impractical for some. Volunteers suggest that you buy an umbrella in-country and stay inside until storms pass.

Shoes
- 1 pair of sneakers or sturdy walking shoes
- 1 pair of rubber-sole flip-flops for bathing
- 1 pair of dress shoes (for swearing-in or other special occasions; for women, dress sandals or ballet flats. You will not need high heels and, if you do, you can always buy them here.)
- 1 pair of sandals (only women should plan to wear nice sandals outside the home; no sandals for men or women in work settings)
- 1 pair of work/hiking boots (practical, waterproof, and comfortable to walk in; particularly helpful for campo projects)

Note: During rainy periods, leather goods accumulate mildew so bring leather-protection cream or milk oil.

Personal Hygiene and Toiletry Items

Many specialty soaps, shampoo, lotion, etc. are available in country (bring a small supply of any <u>special</u> items from the States; women should be advised tampons are very expensive and hard to find here.)

Miscellaneous

Needed Items

- Sturdy backpack/day pack (with enough room for three days' light packing)
- Travel alarm clock
- Flashlight or headlamp
- Towel and washcloth (bring a start-up set; purchase more once you are settled, travel style/size)
- Inexpensive watch (helpful if water-resistant with an alarm and light)
- Small locks for backpacks and luggage

Note: Please bring to El Salvador a Spanish dictionary (new or used). You will need it for PST language classes.

Useful Items
- Pocketknife
- Portable radio/CD/MP3 and/or small speakers
- Shortwave radio
- Flash drive
- Camera
- Money belt (wearable under clothing)
- Cards, backgammon, other games
- Sewing kit
- Water bottle
- Sleeping bag or sleep sack (lightweight; some Volunteers use them, others do not)
- World map
- Cooking spices (basic spices are available, but bring specialty spices if you enjoy cooking)

Recreation

Books and Magazines

Most Volunteers are, or become, avid readers. English language books and magazines are available in the capital for purchase, but are expensive and of a limited selection. You may arrange to have books mailed to you. Packages labeled "LIBROS" usually get through customs. The Volunteer lounges in the main and regional offices have book exchanges with diverse reading material and always welcomes donations from current and departing Volunteers. Subscriptions to magazines may get through, but probably quite late.

Many Volunteers choose to purchase an e-reader (such as a Kindle or Nook) to bring to El Salvador. Bringing extra electronics is an added risk, but they are useful in that you will always have access to a large selection of books. Some PCVs are able to check their email on their e-readers that come with 3G access.

Music

Many Volunteers bring radio or MP3 players with them and greatly appreciate the sanctuary personal music provides. It's suggested that you bringyour favorite music from home, either in CD or MP3 form. Batteries are not cheap, and you may choose to use solar-powered or electrical rechargers.

Laptops are highly recommended by Volunteers (the smaller the better for travel and security)

Photography

Digital cameras are almost a must item. Most Volunteers bring digital cameras. Digital photos can be developed in-country but expensive, and may also be downloaded to the Internet to be shared with family and friends back home.

Note: The climate here may also ruin some of your belongings. For this reason, do not bring things you cannot risk losing due to theft, loss, moisture, etc. Please do not bring high-priced items with you and most definitely do not have them mailed to you. El Salvador is a poor country. You will appear rich or at least affluent to many Salvadorans. The Peace Corps does not provide paid insurance coverage for your personal effects, although you may purchase insurance for your belongings (this will be discussed at your pre-departure orientation). Ultimately, each Volunteer is responsible for the safekeeping of his or her personal belongings. The Peace Corps cannot reimburse you for losses.

Work Supplies

You may need a few basic reference books and supplies for your field of work. You may bring books with you, or preferably, wait until you see what resources Peace Corps/El Salvador may provide. Peace Corps/El Salvador can also order work-related materials through Peace Corps/headquarters. Basic work and art supplies, such as scissors, crayons, markers, and calculators, may be squeezed into your luggage but are also readily available in-country.

Medicines and Related Items

You will receive a basic medical kit as soon as you arrive in-country. Medical treatment and supplies are available at the training center and Peace Corps office. The Peace Corps also provides contraceptives to Volunteers who request them. A variety of over-the-counter medications are provided, as well as any medications prescribed by a Peace Corps physician. It is not necessary to bring a two-year supply. As mentioned, do bring a three-month supply of any medications you need immediately upon arrival, in addition to your prescription. This will allow Peace Corps/El Salvador time to order your medication. This three-month supply will ensure that you have a continuous supply.

Packing

- ALL luggage should be lockable, with airport-approved locks.
  - PUT loose items in something that can be used later, such as boxes, zip-close bags, Tupperware, etc.
  - MARK all of your luggage and equipment inside and out
  - KEEP most of your clothes in one bag and enough items for three days to be used upon arrival in El Salvador
- Trainees should be encouraged to bring small gifts for their host families, such as calendars with pictures featuring their home state or a region.

PRE-DEPARTURE CHECKLIST

The following list consists of suggestions for you to consider as you prepare to live outside the United States for two years. Not all items will be relevant to everyone, and the list does not include everything you should make arrangements for.

Family

- Notify family that they can call the Peace Corps Counseling and Outreach Unit at any time if there is a critical illness or death of a family member (24-hour telephone number: 855.855.1961 ext. 1470).

- Give the Peace Corps On the Home Front handbook to family and friends.

Passport/Travel

- Forward to the Peace Corps travel office all paperwork for the Peace Corps passport and visas.

- Verify that your luggage meets the size and weight limits for international travel.

- Obtain a personal passport if you plan to travel after your service ends. (Your Peace Corps passport will expire three months after you finish your service, so if you plan to travel longer, you will need a regular passport.)

Medical/Health

- Complete any needed dental and medical work.

- If you wear glasses, bring two pairs.

- Arrange to bring a three-month supply of all medications (including birth control pills) you are currently taking.

Insurance

- Make arrangements to maintain life insurance coverage.

- Arrange to maintain supplemental health coverage while you are away. (Even though the Peace Corps is responsible for your health care during Peace Corps service overseas, it is advisable for people who have pre-existing conditions to arrange for the continuation of their supplemental health coverage. If there is a lapse in coverage, it is often difficult and expensive to be reinstated.)

- Arrange to continue Medicare coverage if applicable.

Personal Papers

- Bring a copy of your certificate of marriage or divorce.

Voting

- Register to vote in the state of your home of record. (Many state universities consider voting and payment of state taxes as evidence of residence in that state.)

- Obtain a voter registration card and take it with you overseas.

- Arrange to have an absentee ballot forwarded to you overseas.

Personal Effects

- Purchase personal property insurance to extend from the time you leave your home for service overseas until the time you complete your service and return to the United States.

Financial Management

- Keep a bank account in your name in the U.S.

- Obtain student loan deferment forms from the lender or loan service.

- Execute a Power of Attorney for the management of your property and business and any personal mail (e.g., outstanding bills).

- Arrange for deductions from your readjustment allowance to pay alimony, child support, and other debts through the Office of Volunteer Financial Operations at 855.855.1961 ext. 1770.

- Place all important papers—mortgages, deeds, stocks, and bonds—in a safe deposit box or with an attorney or other caretaker.

CONTACTING PEACE CORPS HEADQUARTERS

This list of numbers will help connect you with the appropriate office at Peace Corps headquarters to answer various questions. You can use the toll-free number and extension or dial directly using the local numbers provided. Be sure to leave the toll-free number and extensions with your family so they can contact you in the event of an emergency.

Peace Corps headquarters toll-free number: 855.855.1961 press 1, then extension # (see below)

Peace Corps mailing address: Peace Corps
Paul D. Coverdell Peace Corps Headquarters
1111 20th Street NW
Washington, DC 20526

For Questions About:	Staff:	Toll-Free Ext:	Direct/Local Number:
Responding to an Invitation:	Office of Placement	ext. 1840	202.692.1840
Country Information:	Monica Suber	ext. 2522	202.692.2522
	Desk Officer	msuber@peacecorps.gov	

Plane Tickets, Passports, Visas, or other travel matters:

	CWT SATO Travel	ext. 1170	202.692.1170
Legal Clearance:	Office of Placement	ext. 1840	202.692.1840

Medical Clearance and Forms Processing (includes dental):

	Screening Nurse	ext. 1500	202.692.1500
Medical Reimbursements (handled by a subcontractor):			800.818.8772
Loan Deferments, Taxes, Financial Operations:		ext. 1770	202.692.1770

Readjustment Allowance Withdrawals, Power of Attorney, Staging (Pre-Departure Orientation), and Reporting Instructions:

	Office of Staging	ext. 1865	202.692.1865

Note: You will receive comprehensive information (hotel and flight arrangements three to five weeks prior to departure. This information is not available sooner).

Family Emergencies (to get information to a Volunteer overseas) *24 hours:*

	Counseling and Outreach Unit	ext. 1470	202.692.1470